WEEKLY READER BOOKS presents

What Is a Dinosaur?

A **Just Ask**™ Book

Hi, my name is Christopher!

D1011490

by Chris Arvetis
and Carole Palmer

illustrated by
James Buckley

FIELD PUBLICATIONS
MIDDLETOWN, CT.

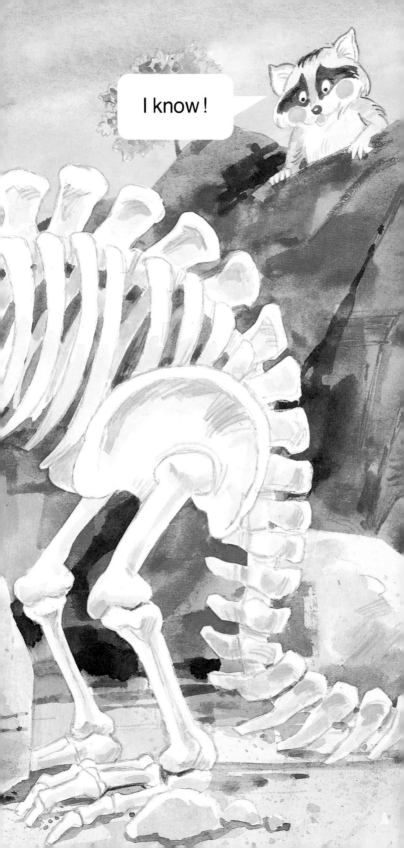

The word dinosaur means "terrible lizard."

The dinosaurs were big and frightening, so they looked terrible.

But they really weren't lizards.

Let me tell you about dinosaurs.

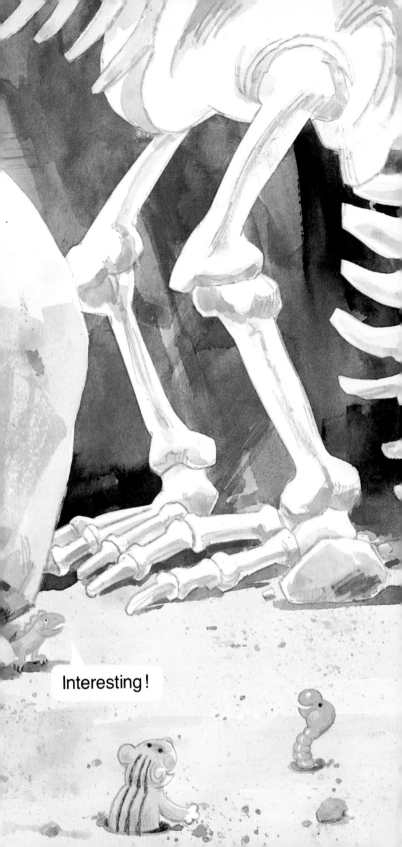

Dinosaurs lived on the earth many millions of years ago.
That's a very, very long time ago.
We can learn about long ago from scientists who study the earth.

Hi!

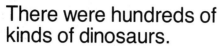

There were hundreds of kinds of dinosaurs.

They came in all shapes and sizes.

But no one knows what color they were.

Dinosaurs could have been colorful with spots and stripes, or they could have been dull and plain.

This is one of the
giant dinosaurs.
It was 70 feet long and
weighed over 40 tons.
Its name means
"thunder lizard."
It may have been named that
because it sounded like
thunder when it walked.

Thunder lizard ?

BRONTOSAURUS

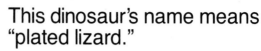

This dinosaur's name means "plated lizard."

It had bony plates on its back.

Two pairs of spikes were on its tail.

The dinosaur would swing its tail to protect itself from other fierce dinosaurs.

This dinosaur walked on its four legs and ate plants.

LAMBESAURUS

TRICERATOPS

There are no more dinosaurs living on earth today.
But, we can see some close relatives in alligators, lizards, and some birds.